Escape Room Adventures

SHERLOCK'S
Greatest Case

Written by Alex Woolf

Illustrated by Sian James

ARCTURUS

ARCTURUS

This edition published in 2024 by Arcturus Publishing
Limited
26/27 Bickels Yard, 151–153 Bermondsey Street,
London SE1 3HA

Author: Alex Woolf
Illustrator: Sian James
Designer: Sarah Fountain
Editor: Violet Peto
Design Manager: Jessica Holliland
Managing Editor: Joe Harris

The publisher would like to say a special thank you to
Rowan for testing the puzzles.

ISBN: 978-1-3988-2564-2
CH010111NT
Supplier 29, Date 0524,, PI 00007325

Printed in China

Welcome to Escape Room Adventures!

The year is 1895. The place, 221b Baker Street, London. You are Sherlock Holmes, the world's most brilliant detective, and, together with your faithful companion Watson, you are about to embark on your greatest adventure!

In the course of this adventure, you will have to test your wits against the notorious criminal mastermind, James Moriarty, by solving a series of puzzles.

Moriarty has stolen the famous Musgrave Diamond from the Baskerville Museum. He knows you are after him, and he will do his best to evade you.

The London Reporter

MUSGRAVE DIAMOND STOLEN!

It is up to you and Watson to find out where Moriarty is, retrieve the diamond, and return it to the museum.

How to Read This Book

Unlike most books, you won't be reading this one from front to back. You must find your own route through the book to solve the mystery. For each puzzle, you are offered three or four possible solutions. Once you think you know the correct one, turn to the entry indicated in the text and see if you're right. Use your observation, lateral thinking, and logic skills to uncover clues and solve the mysteries. The illustrations are packed with information, so keep your eyes peeled!

Difficulty levels

Choose your difficulty level, then race against the clock to solve the mystery!

 ROOKIE DETECTIVE: You have two and a half hours to solve all the puzzles. You also have five lives, which means you're allowed to get the answers wrong up to four times.

 SEASONED SLEUTH: You have two hours to solve all the puzzles and four lives. Get more than three answers wrong, and you have to start again!

MASTER OF DEDUCTION: You have an hour and a half to solve all the puzzles, and three lives, so you can't afford to make many mistakes!

Secret symbols

 Safe to enter

 Dangerous people

 This leads nowhere

 Guard dog

 When you see this symbol, make sure that you observe the person or object indicated very carefully. You will need to remember details later on.

 This time-stop symbol buys you an extra five minutes of puzzle-solving time—should you need it!

Look out for these symbols, which have been left around by your young allies, the Baker Street Irregulars.

Use this wheel to help you decode letter substitution codes. Find each letter in your coded message on the outside of the wheel. Then match it to its corresponding letter on the inside.

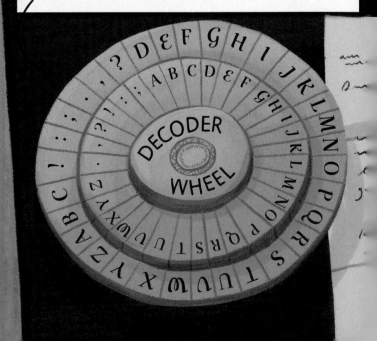

WANTED

MORIARTY

Dancing men code

A	B	C	D	E	F	G	H	I	J	K	L	M

N	O	P	Q	R	S	T	U	V	W	X	Y	Z

This is used for several messages in this book. Here's the key so you can decipher the messages.

Use the table below to help decode messages with numbers substituted for letters, or vice versa.

A	B	C	D	E	F	G	H	I	J	K	L	M
1	2	3	4	5	6	7	8	9	10	11	12	13

N	O	P	Q	R	S	T	U	V	W	X	Y	Z
14	15	16	17	18	19	20	21	22	23	24	25	26

Map of Moriarty's Secret Lair

Secret entrance

Secret access

DINING ROOM

MEETING ROOM

KITCHEN

TREASURY X (diamond)

LIVING ROOM

Secret passage

BEDROOM

Secret access

BATH-ROOM

LIBRARY

ENTRANCE HALL

WEAPONS ROOM

Secret passage

Cave entrance

1

The famous Musgrave Diamond has been stolen! You hurry along to the scene of the theft at the Baskerville Museum. You investigate the scene in search of clues. Near the smashed glass display case, you find a dropped glove. At the museum's lost property office, you find several more odd gloves.

A

B

C

D

Can you find the matching glove you found among this assortment of gloves?

If your answer is A, turn to entry 65.

If your answer is B, turn to entry 14.

If your answer is C, turn to entry 18.

If your answer is D, turn to entry 133.

2 I'm afraid that one won't take you down to the cave roof. Lose a life and climb back to entry 21.

3 That's not Peterson's phone number. Lose a life and dial back to entry 61.

4 That is not the man handing a note to Christa Belle. Lose a life and go back to entry 103.

5 You break the code and discover the message is KEY IN ODD NAPOLEON. What can that mean? You continue to explore Moriarty's lair. In the library, you find a shelf containing four plaster busts of the great French general Napoleon Bonaparte. You realize that a key Christa Belle needs must be inside one of these—the odd one. Which one could that be?

If your answer is A, turn to entry 12.

If your answer is B, turn to entry 158.

If your answer is C, turn to entry 106.

If your answer is D, turn to entry 61.

6 That key does not match the chalk outline. Lose a life and go back to entry 166.

7 That is not the man you can see in silhouette. Lose a life, check your eyesight, and return to entry 72.

8

You were right. It's Peterson, your friend. He's coming to help you get away. You are safe! You begin your journey back to London.

At Calais, you bid farewell to Peterson and hire a steamboat to take you across the Channel. Your boat has a blue and yellow flag, an orange hull, and one R in its name. Can you see which one it is?

A

LIBERTY

B

SERENDIPITY

CARPE DIEM

C

AURORA

D

If your answer is A, turn to entry 185.

If your answer is B, turn to entry 32.

If your answer is C, turn to entry 83.

If your answer is D, turn to entry 55.

9

That is not the correct door, I'm afraid. Lose a life and go back to entry 15.

10

You have failed to identify the fake note. Lose a life and go back to entry 144.

11

You remember he is Colonel Moran. You watch him write a note, then place it inside a book. He looks at the book and chuckles to himself: "Four letters occur exactly twice each in this title, and another one occurs exactly three times." Then he returns it to the shelf and leaves the room. You hurry to retrieve the book. On the basis of Moran's clue, find the book. On which shelf is it?

If you think it's on the top shelf, turn to entry 119.

If you think it's on the second shelf, turn to entry 71.

If you think it's on the third shelf, turn to entry 180.

If you think it's on the bottom shelf, turn to entry 57.

12
You chose the wrong Napoleon. Lose a life and troop back to entry 5.

13
That was not the symbol on the tile. Lose a life and go back to entry 75.

14
That was not the matching glove. Lose a life and return to entry 1.

15

"Congratulations!" Moriarty's voice booms. "You have reached the final room. Get this one right and you will be free. Here are four identical doors, but only one will lead you out of this building. I'm afraid your deductive skills won't help you this time, Holmes. You're simply going to have to take a guess!" His laughter echoes around the room. You bend to take a closer look and spot some very faint marks on the doors. The Baker Street Irregulars must have been here. Can you see which door will lead you to safety?

A   B   C   D

If your answer is A, turn to entry 93.

If your answer is B, turn to entry 207.

If your answer is C, turn to entry 9.

If your answer is D, turn to entry 168.

16
That was the wrong piece, I'm afraid. Lose a life and go back to entry 47.

17
That is not the woman's name. Lose a life and go back to entry 64.

18 You find the store that sells these gloves on London's Regent Street. The clerk looks up the address of the customer in his ledger, but it makes no sense. You quickly realize it's been written in a letter substitution code. Can you decrypt it?

73 Phooedqh Urdg, Vrxwkjdwh

If your answer is 73 Mellbane Road, Southgate, turn to entry 72.

If your answer is 73 Mellbure Road, Northgate, turn to entry 102.

If your answer is 73 Mellburn Road, Northwall, turn to entry 49.

If your answer is 73 Mellvane Road, Southport, turn to entry 199.

19 That rope will not take you safely to the ground. Lose a life and climb back to entry 152.

20 That woman is too tall! Lose a life and go back to entry 107.

21 You worked out which footprints belonged to Christa Belle and have followed the path to Mount Reichenbach. The cave entrance is well guarded. Nearby is a ski lift. If you cut its cables, you can climb down one of these to the cave roof without the guard noticing. But the cables get tangled.

Which one will take you closest to the cave roof?

If your answer is A, turn to entry 2.

If your answer is B, turn to entry 160.

If your answer is C, turn to entry 103.

A

B

C

22 I'm afraid that won't reassemble the tile correctly. Lose a life and go back to entry 141.

23 Those are not the correct symbols to make sense of the sum. Lose a life and recalculate your way back to entry 117.

24 Those are not the correct coordinates. Lose a life and navigate your route back to entry 138.

25 You enter through the window of Moriarty's bedroom. Behind a wardrobe you find a large steel door. This could be the safe where he keeps the diamond. There is a four-digit combination lock on the door. To figure out the code you need to solve the equations below, solving the sums as they appear from left to right. Then, rearrange the numbers into ascending order.

$$3 + 4 \times 2 - 6 =$$
$$6 - 5 + 1 \times 3 =$$
$$4 \times 4 - 9 + 2 =$$
$$7 + 3 \times 5 - 47 =$$

If your answer is 9-8-6-3, turn to entry 191.
If your answer is 3-6-8-9, turn to entry 79.
If your answer is 2-3-8-9, turn to entry 110.
If your answer is 5-6-8-9, turn to entry 31.

26 Your memory for names is not all it should be. Lose a life and go back to entry 114.

27 Your word-searching skills need a little work. Lose a life and go back to entry 193.

28 I'm afraid that wasn't the quickest route from London to Paris. Lose a life and take a return trip to entry 86.

There are four keys to the cabinet. Which one matches the outline drawn on the door?

If your answer is A, turn to entry 174.

If your answer is B, turn to entry 163.

If your answer is C, turn to entry 78.

If your answer is D, turn to entry 52.

30 You're not getting the picture, are you? Lose a life and go back to entry 131.

31 That combination won't open any doors for you. Lose a life and swing back to entry 25.

32 You found the correct boat. You go to the Baskerville Museum and return the diamond to its rightful place. You inform the police about Moriarty's secret mountain lair, and a few days later you receive news of his arrest, along with Colonel Moran, Jack Stapleton, and the rest of his gang.

CONGRATULATIONS! You have completed your mission.

33 That is not the correct window, I'm afraid. Lose a life and climb back down to entry 127.

34 That is not your guide's name. Lose a life and find your way back to entry 173.

35 That city does not contain the Colosseum. Lose a life and travel back to entry 204.

36

Phew! You defused the bomb and the train arrives safely in Rome. Now you need to get to Moriarty's hideout before Christa Belle. His base is on the corner of Via dei Serpenti and Via Irene Adler. What is the quickest route?

A: Wait for tram: 6 minutes, 54 seconds; Tram ride: 7 minutes, 45 seconds; Walk: 2 minutes, 21 seconds

B: Walk to destination: 16 minutes, 50 seconds

C: Wait for horse bus: 3 minutes, 11 seconds; Horse bus ride: 9 minutes, 49 seconds; Walk: 3 minutes, 55 seconds

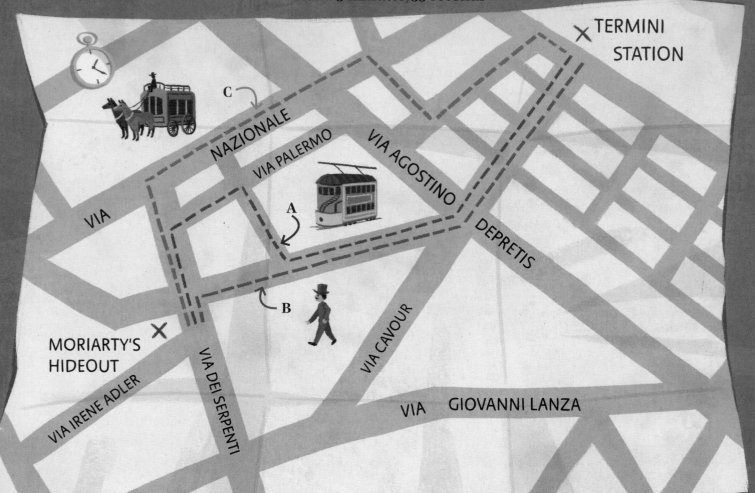

37
That was the wrong fingerprint. Lose a life and go back to entry 54.

38
That is not what the secret message said. Lose a life and go back to entry 100.

If your answer is A, turn to entry 184.

If your answer is B, turn to entry 51.

If your answer is C, turn to entry 137.

39
You might need to work on your jigsaw puzzle skills. That is not the correct order for reassembling the tile. Lose a life and go back to entry 141.

40

You remember the name of the mountain. In the library, you discover that Mount Reichenbach is in the Swiss Alps near the village of Meiringen. You rush to the railway station and consult the timetables. How long will it take you to get there by train if the average time taken at each station stop is 12 minutes?

TRENI IN PARTENZA

Rome to Milan: 4 hours, 13 minutes.

Milan to Lugano: 2 hours, 34 minutes.

Lugano to Luzern: 1 hour, 41 minutes.

Luzern to Meiringen: 1 hour, 2 minutes.

If you think it will take 10 hours, 6 minutes, turn to entry 173.

If you think it will take 9 hours, 56 minutes, turn to entry 56.

If you think it will take 10 hours, 18 minutes, turn to entry 140.

If you think it will take 10 hours, 2 minutes, turn to entry 128.

41 Whoops! You chose the wrong route across the floor of the treasury. Lose a life and reverse back to entry 68.

42 No, the secret passage is not behind there. Lose a life, recheck the map, and go back to entry 200.

43 You put out the wrong fuse, and the bomb is about to go off! Lose a life and dash back to entry 90.

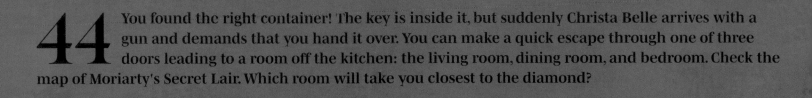

44 You found the right container! The key is inside it, but suddenly Christa Belle arrives with a gun and demands that you hand it over. You can make a quick escape through one of three doors leading to a room off the kitchen: the living room, dining room, and bedroom. Check the map of Moriarty's Secret Lair. Which room will take you closest to the diamond?

If you think it's the living room, turn to entry 94.

If you think it's the dining room, turn to entry 126.

If you think it's the bedroom, turn to entry 68.

45 That bird's-eye view does not match Moriarty's building. Lose a life and float back to entry 97.

46 I'm afraid that pattern does not complete the sequence. Lose a life and return to entry 169.

47

You enter the correct door and find yourself in an empty room. On the floor is a piece of paper that's been torn into pieces. It looks like a map. You're sure it will give you a clue, so you put it back together.

It's a map of Europe. One piece is missing, but there are several pieces that could fit. Which one is it?

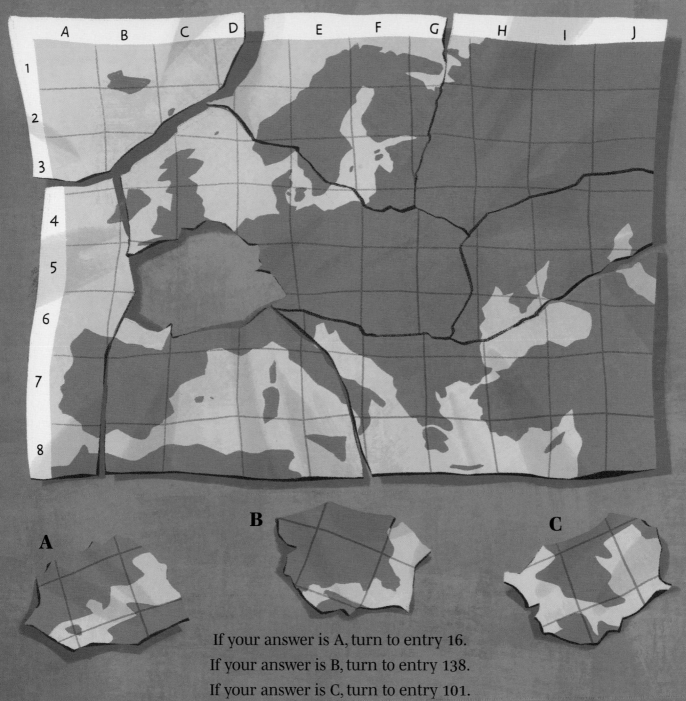

If your answer is A, turn to entry 16.

If your answer is B, turn to entry 138.

If your answer is C, turn to entry 101.

48 That is not the quickest route from London to Paris. Lose a life and take a return trip to entry 86.

49 That is not the correct address. Lose a life and find your way back to entry 18.

50 That is not Moriarty, you may be relieved to know! Lose a life and go back to entry 163.

51 You realize that it's quickest to walk to Moriarty's base, and this is lucky because you get there just in time to see Christa Belle enter a five-character code. Your view is blocked but you see enough to know that the code contains the number 9, and there are two letters from the top row. Now you must try to work out the code she entered. You saw the beginning of it when you saw Christa Belle taking a coded message out of an envelope. Can you remember it?

0 1 2 3 4 5 6 7 8 9
A B C D E F G H I
J K L M N O P Q R
S T U V W X Y Z

If you think it's B 6 W 9 P, turn to entry 80.
If you think it's 8 F 3 H 9, turn to entry 62.
If you think it's 6 B 9 F 2, turn to entry 75.
If you think it's 8 D 7 B 0, turn to entry 151.

52 That key does not match the outline. Lose a life and go back to entry 29.

53 I'm afraid those are not the map coordinates. Lose a life and navigate your way back to entry 93.

54

You board the quickest train to Rome. On the train, you spot the woman you saw earlier at the café, this time without her disguise. You want to know who she is. You steal her glass from the dining car and lift a fingerprint from it, which you compare to the prints of some famous female criminals. Which one is it?

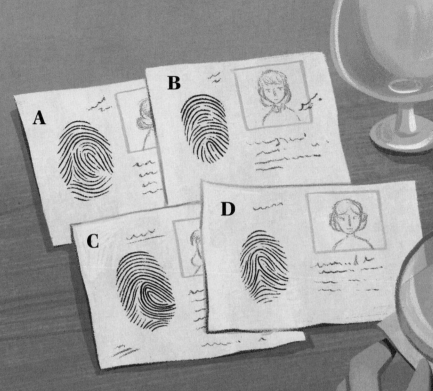

If your answer is A, turn to entry 122.

If your answer is B, turn to entry 37.

If your answer is C, turn to entry 76.

If your answer is D, turn to entry 64.

55
You chose the wrong boat. Lose a life and voyage back to entry 8.

56
You got the journey time wrong. Lose a life and buy a return ticket to entry 40.

57
You chose the wrong bookshelf. Lose a life and flip back to entry 11.

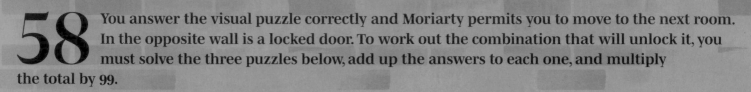

58

You answer the visual puzzle correctly and Moriarty permits you to move to the next room. In the opposite wall is a locked door. To work out the combination that will unlock it, you must solve the three puzzles below, add up the answers to each one, and multiply the total by 99.

In Olympus there is a tree that grows golden apples. Heracles eats three, Athena eats four, Leto eats two and gives three to each of her children, Apollo and Artemis. There are five apples left on the tree. How many were there to begin with?

During your journey you spend 207 minutes in a train, 15 minutes in a cab, and 18 minutes on foot. How many hours in total does your journey last?

In Stradivarius' workshop, five apprentices can make 20 violins in 10 days. How many days will it take 10 apprentices to make 80 violins?

He's toying with us, Watson, as a cat toys with a mouse!

If your answer is 3-4-6-5, turn to entry 67.

If your answer is 4-3-5-6, turn to entry 193.

If your answer is 2-8-7-1, turn to entry 116.

59
You failed to recognize the silhouette. Lose a life and go back to entry 177.

60
Those are the wrong footprints. Lose a life and trudge back to entry 183.

61

You correctly identify the "odd Napoleon" and you smash it on the floor, but there's no key inside. Instead, there's a note with Peterson's name on it and a telephone number. However, the numbers are jumbled.

Solve the clues to work out the correct order of numbers.

The first, second, and fifth digits are prime numbers.

The first and second digits add up to eight.

The fourth digit is five more than the third.

The first digit is lower than the sixth.

**PETERSON
654321**

If your answer is 251634, turn to entry 149.
If your answer is 351624, turn to entry 200.
If your answer is 531624, turn to entry 3.

62
You have not remembered the code correctly. Lose a life, work on that memory, and flash back to entry 51.

63
Your decoding skills need some work! Lose a life and go back to entry 180.

64

You correctly identify her fingerprint and discover that she lists her name as CIALHSBLRTEE. This has to be in code. You try writing her name vertically in three columns, four letters to a column, and then read it horizontally across each row. What does it spell out?

If your answer is Charlie Brett, turn to entry 136.
If your answer is Lilac Sherbet, turn to entry 157.
If your answer is Christa Belle, turn to entry 144.
If your answer is Elsbeth Caril, turn to entry 17.

65
You chose the wrong glove. Lose a life and go back to entry 1.

66
You took the wrong route through the maze. Lose a life and sneak back to entry 155.

67
That was the wrong combination. Lose a life and go back to entry 58.

68

You run to the bedroom: a wise choice. There is a secret access between the bedroom and the treasury, the location of the diamond.

You use the key to open the treasury door, then lock yourselves in. The room is filled with stolen treasure! The Musgrave Diamond is alone in a glass case at the far end of the room. A sign tells you how to cross the floor with out setting off an alarm.

YOU MUST STEP ON TILES IN THIS ORDER:

Which route will take you there? You may move forward, backward, left, and right, but not diagonally.

A   B   C

If you choose route A, turn to entry 41.
If you choose route B, turn to entry 139.
If you choose route C, turn to entry 117.

69
I'm afraid that escape route will not work! Lose a life and sneak back to entry 124.

70
That is not what the message is telling you. Lose a life and slurp your way back to entry 100.

71
You chose the wrong book on the wrong bookshelf! Lose a life and flick back to entry 11.

72 You successfully decode the message and discover it is the address of a house in Southgate, North London. You take a hansom cab there. No one answers your knock, so you break in through a rear window. In the living room, you catch sight of a silhouette. Which one of Moriarty's accomplices does the shape most resemble?

A

B

C

If your answer is A, turn to entry 203.

If your answer is B, turn to entry 196.

If your answer is C, turn to entry 7.

73 That was not the correct shelf, I'm afraid! Lose a life and go back to entry 148.

74 You failed to decode the message correctly. Lose a life and return to the cell in entry 100.

Well done! You remembered the code. You enter the building and find yourself in a hallway. There are three doors at the far end, each marked by a slightly different symbol. Which one was the symbol on the clay tile you found on the train?

A

B

C

If you think it's Door A, turn to entry 169.
If you think it's Door B, turn to entry 13.
If you think it's Door C, turn to entry 197.

76 That is not the correct fingerprint. Lose a life, polish your magnifying glass, and go back to entry 54.

77 If you take that route, you'll set off the alarm! Lose a life and hurry back to entry 79.

78 That key will not fit the ski cabinet. Lose a life and go back to entry 29.

79

You manage to open the steel door. Behind it is a room containing an ornate box, which you think could contain the stolen diamond. To reach it, you must cross a booby-trapped floor. You can only step on squares that are multiples of six, or you will set off an alarm.

12	55	90	37	50	24	14	64
6	7	54	39	90	73	4	59
52	61	29	66	27	19	26	93
11	84	6	63	86	33	10	35
48	29	47	72	83	78	40	9
8	56	39	18	24	42	60	92
31	13	28	54	48	1	45	66
19	87	15	36	12	85	25	6

A   B   C

Which route must you take to get across the room?

If your answer is A, turn to entry 77.

If your answer is B, turn to entry 155.

If your answer is C, turn to entry 129.

80 You didn't remember the code. Lose a life and go back to entry 51.

81 That's not what the message said, I'm afraid! Lose a life and go back to entry 120.

So Moriarty is no longer in Paris. He must have fled to Rome with the diamond. Which of the following trains will get you from Paris to Rome the quickest? Each station stop adds twelve minutes to the journey.

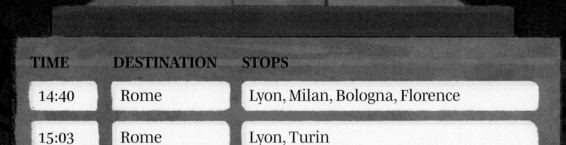

TIME	DESTINATION	STOPS
14:40	Rome	Lyon, Milan, Bologna, Florence
15:03	Rome	Lyon, Turin
15:30	Rome	

If your answer is 14.40, turn to entry 182.

If your answer is 15.03, turn to entry 54.

If your answer is 15.30, turn to entry 95.

83 I'm sorry to say that's the wrong boat. Lose a life and steam back to entry 8.

84 That is not the right order. Lose a life and return to entry 141.

85 That is not the name of the man. Lose a life and go back to entry 103.

86

You've worked out that Moriarty has gone to Paris, France. What is the quickest route from London to Paris?

If you think it's quickest to depart from Charing Cross, turn to entry 187.

If you think it's quickest to depart from Cannon Street, turn to entry 48.

If you think it's quickest to depart from Victoria, turn to entry 28.

TIMETABLE.

LONDON–PARIS LINE

		Hours	Minutes
Charing Cross → Folkestone		1	55
Folkestone → Boulogne		2	20
Boulogne → Paris		4	2
Cannon Street → Dover		1	45
Dover → Calais		2	16
Calais → Paris		4	30
Victoria → Newhaven		1	56
Newhaven → Dieppe		4	12
Dieppe → Paris		2	51

87
You got the numbers wrong, I'm afraid! Lose a life and go back to entry 159.

88
Your memory for mountain names is a little shaky! Lose a life and go back to entry 111.

89
You picked the wrong window. Lose a life and climb back to entry 127.

You've managed to reassemble the tile. Meanwhile, Christa Belle has escaped by leaping off the train—and she's left a bomb on board! There are three burning fuses but only one connects to the bomb, and they're all tangled up. Which fuse should you cut?

A   B   C

If your answer is A, turn to entry 161.
If your answer is B, turn to entry 43.
If your answer is C, turn to entry 36.

91 You chose the wrong panel. Lose a life and go back to entry 196.

92 Those are not the coordinates of the mountain. Lose a life and go back to entry 93.

93

You passed Moriarty's final test. You open the door and it leads into the street. But Moriarty's guards quickly arrive and capture you, forcing you back into the building and down some steps into a cell. You should have known Moriarty wouldn't play by the rules of his own game!

Christa Belle is there, also imprisoned. She says Moriarty is keeping the diamond in a secret lair beneath a mountain. She pulls out a map of Europe. She has two clues to the mountain's coordinates. The letter is three back from G. The number is the solution to the following equation reading from left to right: 2 x 9 ÷ 3. Can you work out the coordinates?

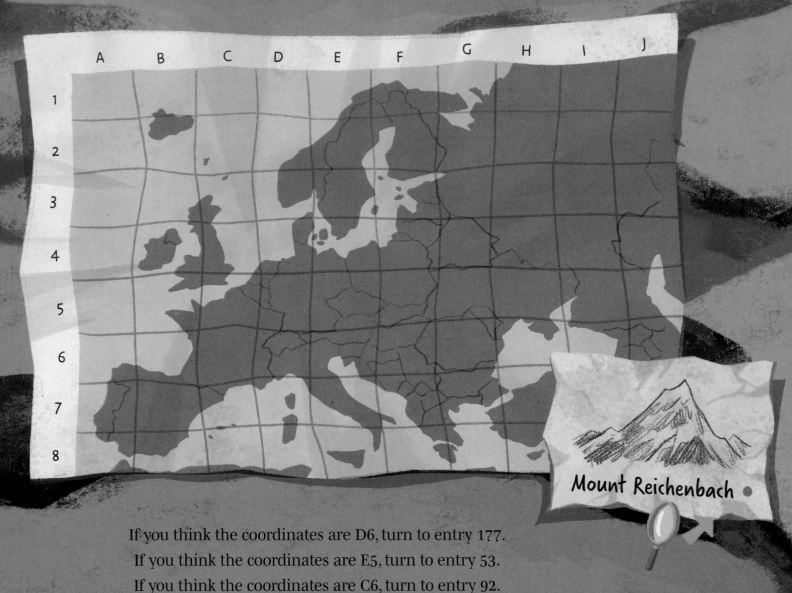

Mount Reichenbach

If you think the coordinates are D6, turn to entry 177.

If you think the coordinates are E5, turn to entry 53.

If you think the coordinates are C6, turn to entry 92.

94
You've chosen the wrong room! Lose a life and run back to entry 44.

95
That was not the fastest train to Rome. Lose a life and take an express trip back to entry 82.

96
I'm afraid you won't find the Colosseum in that city, no matter how hard you look. Lose a life and head back to entry 204.

97

You find Peterson and he gives you a picture of Moriarty's house. The house is well guarded. You take a trip in a hot-air balloon over Paris, hoping to land on the roof of Moriarty's building and take him by surprise. Which of these bird's-eye views is the same as the building in the picture?

I'm worried about this, Watson. We could be venturing into a trap.

A

B

C

If your answer is A, turn to entry 152.
If your answer is B, turn to entry 45.
If your answer is C, turn to entry 135.

98
I'm afraid that is not Christa Belle's footprint. Lose a life and trudge back up the snowy path to entry 183.

99
Sorry, but that is not what the code says. Lose a life and go back to entry 120.

100

You are correct. The man is Peterson. He works for Moriarty, but he's actually your friend. He hands you some food. Under your soup bowl you find a slip of paper with some writing on it. Is it a secret message? What does it say?

Friends, do not despair but look to the future. Don't live under a cloud. There's always hope. The trick is to follow the steps. Every sixth word.

If you think the message is telling you about a person who you can trust, turn to entry 74.

If you think the message is telling you about poison in the food, turn to entry 70.

If you think the message is telling you about when something will happen, turn to entry 38.

If you think the message is telling you about a place to look for something, turn to entry 166.

101
That is not the missing piece, I'm afraid. Lose a life and go back to entry 47.

102
That is not the correct address. Lose a life and send yourself back to entry 18.

103 You climb down the cable that takes you to the cave roof. From here, you are able to crawl through a small space into the cave's entrance hall. You look down to see Christa Belle! A man walks in and hands her a note. You overhear Christa Belle calling him by the codename POLECAT. To discover his real name, you compare the codename to the names of four possible suspects. Which suspect's name contains all the letters of the codename?

If you think it is John Lancer, turn to entry 4.

If you think it is Jean-Paul Dupond, turn to entry 85.

If you think it is Carl Potts, turn to entry 164.

If you think it is Jack Stapleton turn to entry 120.

104 You have failed to decode the message. Lose a life and go back to entry 180.

105 You have failed to identify Peterson. Lose a life and go back to entry 187.

106 That's not the odd Napoleon, I'm afraid. Lose a life and battle your way back to entry 5.

107 You manage to decipher the message correctly. It says "Café Angela, Rue de Rivoli, tomorrow at ten." You go there the next day, and at 10 a.m. Colonel Moran gets up from a table, leaving behind an envelope. Seconds later, a woman arrives and picks up the envelope. Which of these women is she? Remember, she could be in disguise.

If your answer is A, turn to entry 131.

If your answer is B, turn to entry 20.

If your answer is C, turn to entry 153.

108 Sorry, you won't find Moriarty's hideout there. Lose a life and go back to entry 190.

109 That is not the right key. Lose a life and turn back to entry 166.

110 I'm afraid that's not the code for the safe. Lose a life and go back to entry 25.

111 You manage to escape the cell and Moriarty's house. Christa Belle gives you the slip. Do you remember the name of the mountain where she said the diamond is hidden?

If you think it's Rockingbeck, turn to entry 154.
If you think it's Reichenbach, turn to entry 40.
If you think it's Reachenback, turn to entry 88.

112 Those are not the coordinates. Lose a life and go back to entry 138.

113 You've failed to identify the silhouette. Lose a life and glide back to entry 163.

114

Congratulations! You got through the maze. On the far side you find a library. Upon entering, you spot someone in there. It's someone you were told to remember earlier. Can you remember his name?

If you think it was General Moreno, turn to entry 118.

If you think it was Captain Maron, turn to entry 26.

If you think it was Colonel Moran, turn to entry 11.

If you think it was Lieutenant Maroon, turn to entry 130.

115 You chose the wrong escape route! Lose a life and go back to entry 124.

116 That was not the correct combination. Lose a life, brush up on your problem-solving skills, and head back to entry 58.

117

Christa Belle is thumping on the door, demanding to be let in. Outside you hear footsteps crunching in the snow. Moriarty has arrived! To open the glass case, you have to solve a mathematical problem. To solve the equation, insert the correct mathematical symbol in each space. Calculate the equations as they appear by reading from left to right.

You can choose from the following symbols: + - x ÷

$$60 \;\square\; 20 \;\square\; 4 \;\square\; 5 = 100$$

If you think it's + - ÷, turn to entry 188.

If you think it's - x ÷, turn to entry 143.

If you think it's x - +, turn to entry 23.

If you think it's + ÷ x, turn to entry 124.

118
No, the man was not called General Moreno. Lose a life and march back to entry 114.

119
The book was not on that shelf, I'm afraid. Lose a life and speed-read back to entry 11.

120

You correctly identify the man as Jack Stapleton, a thief who has done business with Christa Belle in the past but now works for Moriarty. You pickpocket the note from Christa Belle. On it are some very strange-looking words:

NHB LQ RGG QDSROHRQ

You realize this is a letter substitution code. Can you solve it?

If you think it says DIG TO THE DIAMOND, turn to entry 99.

If you think it says KEY IN ODD NAPOLEON, turn to entry 5.

If you think it says KEY IN THE PAINTING, turn to entry 189.

If you think it says KEY IN THE CUPBOARD, turn to entry 81.

121 That door was not safe to enter! Close it quickly, lose a life, and hurry back to entry 134.

122 That is not the woman's fingerprint. Lose a life and go back to entry 54.

123 Moran is not the missing name. You need to work on those word-searching skills! Lose a life and return to entry 193.

124

Congratulations! You solved the problem and the glass case opens. Now you must escape with the diamond. Christa Belle is in the bedroom. Moriarty and his guards have arrived in the entrance hall. Using the map, can you find a route to escape from the cave without being seen?

A Weapons room, library, kitchen, out through secret entrance at back
B Treasury bedroom, kitchen, out through secret entrance at back
C Weapons room, library, entrance hall, out through front entrance

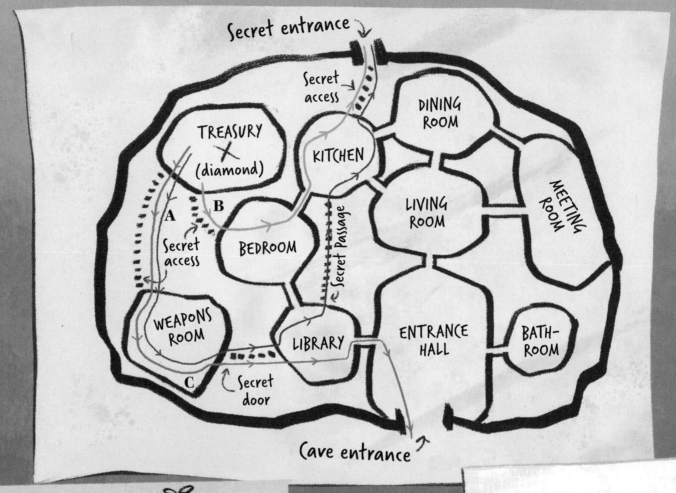

If you choose route A, turn to entry 29.
If you choose route B, turn to entry 69.
If you choose route C, turn to entry 115.

125 You chose the wrong panel. Lose a life and go back to entry 196.

126 That was not the best escape route. Lose a life and hurry back to entry 44.

127 You manage to descend safely to the ground. You must find another way of entering Moriarty's house. You decide to climb up to Moriarty's bedroom window and hope to surprise him that way. Peterson gave you some clues to help you find the correct window.

It has an even number of window panes.

It is next to a window with an odd number of panes.

The window above it has a number of panes that is a square number.

If your answer is A, turn to entry 33.
If your answer is B, turn to entry 146.
If your answer is C, turn to entry 89.
If your answer is D, turn to entry 25.

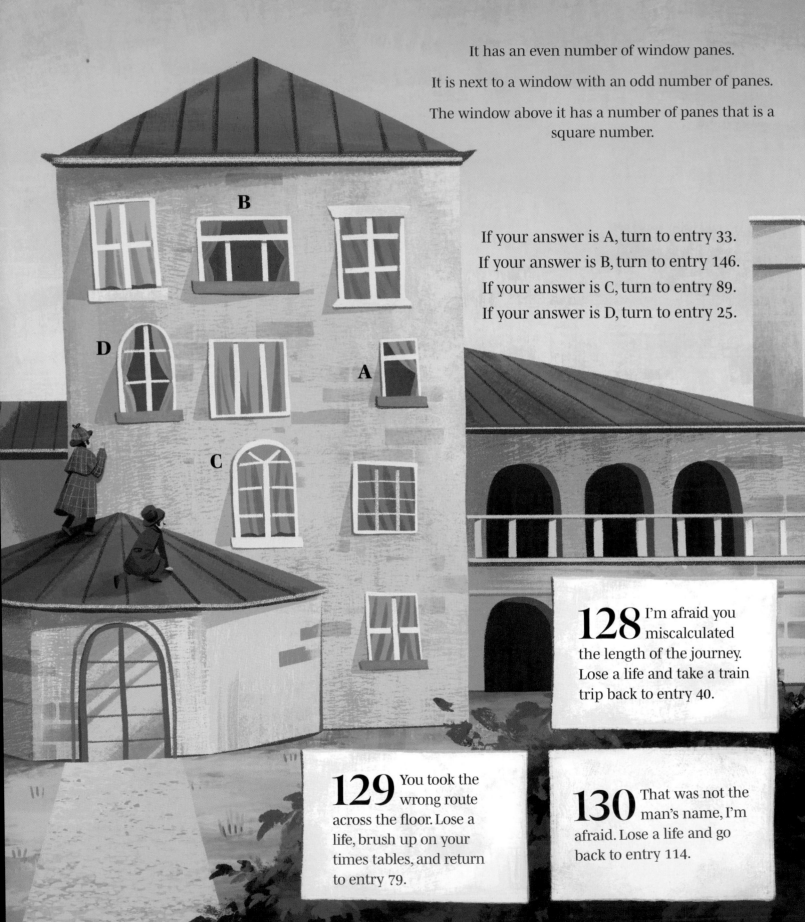

128 I'm afraid you miscalculated the length of the journey. Lose a life and take a train trip back to entry 40.

129 You took the wrong route across the floor. Lose a life, brush up on your times tables, and return to entry 79.

130 That was not the man's name, I'm afraid. Lose a life and go back to entry 114.

131

You correctly identify the woman as someone who has had business dealings with Moriarty in the past. She opens the envelope and takes out a note with a sequence of letters and numbers, but you can only see part of it. Then she takes out a picture, which she looks at, then rips to pieces and tosses away. You race to retrieve the pieces. Can you put them back together in the right order?

What does the hidden message on the picture tell you?

If you think it reveals details of a rendezvous, turn to entry 30.

If you think it tells you someone's whereabouts, turn to entry 204.

If you think it warns you of a trap, turn to entry 186.

132
That was the wrong shelf. Lose a life and go back to entry 148.

133
I'm afraid that was the wrong glove. Lose a life and finger walk back to entry 1.

134

You find the secret door in one of the panels and go through it. On the other side is a set of steps leading down into darkness. You light a candle and walk down the steps. At the bottom is a cellar where you find four doors. Which door is safe to enter?

If your answer is A, turn to entry 121.

If your answer is B, turn to entry 194.

If your answer is C, turn to entry 47.

If your answer is D, turn to entry 206.

135
That was not the same as the building in the picture. Lose a life and take your hot air balloon back to entry 97.

136
Your decoding skills need some work! Lose a life and go back to entry 64.

137
That was not the quickest route to Moriarty's hideout. Lose a life and hurry back to entry 36. There's no time to waste!

138

You've repaired the map. Somewhere on there is Moriarty's current location. Crack the code to find out where he is, then give the map coordinates.

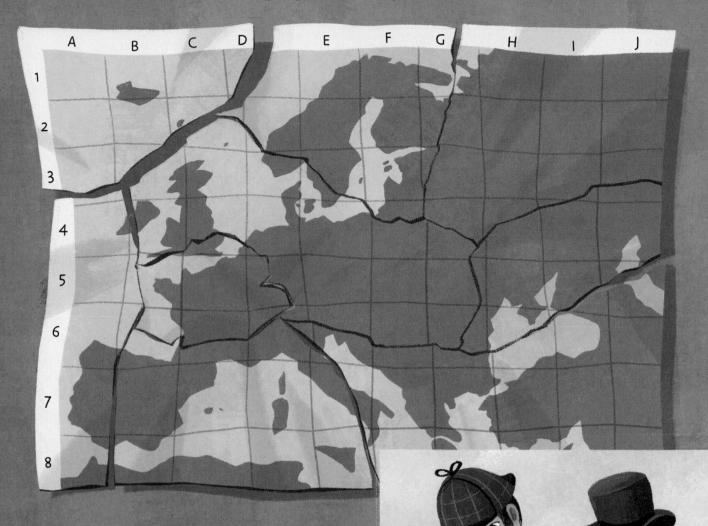

If your answer is F4, turn to entry 162.

If your answer is C5, turn to entry 86.

If your answer is E3, turn to entry 24.

If your answer is F4, turn to entry 112.

139 You chose the wrong route, I'm afraid. Lose a life and go back to entry 68.

140 You miscalculated the journey time. Lose a life and take the express train back to entry 40.

141

You work out that Moriarty's hideout is on the Via dei Serpenti. But then Christa Belle wakes up and sees you with her suitcase. You fight her for it. In the fight, a clay tile drops out of the case and smashes on the floor. Christa Belle runs off with the case. Can you reassemble the tile?

In what order should the numbers be placed, moving row by row, top to bottom, left to right?

If you think it's 4-7-2-9-6-3-1-8-5, turn to entry 90.

If you think it's 7-9-4-1-5-6-3-2-8, turn to entry 39.

If you think it's 4-8-3-6-9-2-1-5-7, turn to entry 84.

If you think it's 1-6-5-4-3-7-8-9-2, turn to entry 22.

142

Sorry, you chose the wrong city! Lose a life and go back to entry 204.

143

Those symbols will not provide you with the right answer. Lose a life and go back to entry 117.

144

Christa Belle, you discover, is a dealer in luxury stolen goods. You think she must be planning to buy the Musgrave Diamond from Moriarty. While she is sleeping, you peek inside her suitcase and find it full of money. You compare one of the notes to some notes from your wallet. You think the note looks fake, but can you be sure?

Which of these is the fake note?

If your answer is A, turn to entry 10.

If your answer is B, turn to entry 190.

If your answer is C, turn to entry 178.

If your answer is D, turn to entry 202.

A

Bank of England

Promise to pay the Bearer on Demand the sum of One Hundred Pounds

ONE HUNDRED   BANK OF ENGLAND

B

Bank of England

Promise to pay the Bearer on Demand the sum of One Hundred Pounds

ONE HUNDRED   BANK OF ENGLAND

C

Bank of England

Promise to pay the Bearer on Demand the sum of One Hundred Pounds

ONE HUNDRED   BANK OF ENGLAND

D

Bank of England

Promise to pay the Bearer on Demand the sum of One Hundred Pounds

ONE HUNDRED   BANK OF ENGLAND

145
I'm afraid that pattern will not complete the sequence. Lose a life and go back to entry 169.

146
You picked the wrong window! Lose a life and climb back to entry 127.

147
Taking that path will not get you through the maze. Lose a life and find your way back to entry 155.

148

You reach the kitchen and find the shelves containing a number of containers. Peterson told you the key was in one of these. Unfortunately, he struggled to remember which one.

He told you it was green, red, and either blue or yellow. He said it had a lid but no handle, and straight sides. He said it was taller than the bell but shorter than the book. Is the correct container on the top, middle, or bottom shelf?

149
That was not the correct ordering of the numbers. Lose a life and go back to entry 61.

150
That rope will not take you to the ground without breaking! Lose a life and hoist yourself back up to entry 152.

151
You failed to remember the code. Lose a life and go back to entry 51.

If you think it's on the top shelf, turn to entry 73.
If you think it's on the middle shelf, turn to entry 132.
If you think it's on the bottom shelf, turn to entry 44.

152

You find Moriarty's building, but a guard on the roof sees you trying to land your balloon and shoots at it. The balloon deflates and crashes into a tree. Four tangled ropes will take you back to the ground, but three of them are frayed. Which is the safe rope?

A   B   C   D

If your answer is A, turn to entry 192.

If your answer is B, turn to entry 150.

If your answer is C, turn to entry 19.

If your answer is D, turn to entry 127.

153
Her disguise must have fooled you! That's not the woman. Lose a life and go back to entry 107.

154
That is not the name of the mountain. Lose a life and go back to entry 111.

155

You successfully cross the room, but when you open the box, you see it's empty! Moriarty must have moved the diamond when he saw you arriving. Suddenly, an alarm sounds. It's a trap! You run out of the room. There are guards everywhere. You sneak down a back staircase to a courtyard containing a maze. Find a route through it that avoids the security guards.

If your answer is A, turn to entry 114.

If your answer is B, turn to entry 66.

If your answer is C, turn to entry 147.

If your answer is D, turn to entry 205.

156
That is not the man's name. Lose a life and go back to entry 173.

157
That is not the woman's name (though it would be funny if it was!). Lose a life and go back to entry 64.

158
You picked the wrong Napoleon! Lose a life and march back to entry 5.

159

You correctly identify the missing name and are permitted to enter the next room, which contains a blackboard and some chalk. "To enter the next room," says Moriarty's voice, "I want you to write down the five numbers I have in my head. Here are your clues ..."

- The numbers add up to twenty-seven.
- The second number is one-third of the total sum of the numbers.
- The fifth number is seven less than the second number.
- The third number is the difference between the second and fifth numbers.
- The first number is two more than the fifth number.

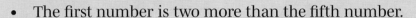

If your answer is 5-8-7-4-3, turn to entry 87.
If your answer is 3-9-8-4-3, turn to entry 198.
If your answer is 4-9-6-3-5, turn to entry 170.
If your answer is 4-9-7-5-2, turn to entry 15.

160
That cable will not take you close to the cave roof. Lose a life and climb back up to entry 21.

161
That fuse does not connect to the bomb. You've wasted valuable time putting it out. Lose a life and blast back to entry 90.

162
Those are the wrong map coordinates. Lose a life and go back to entry 138.

163 Outside it's dark. You start skiing down the mountain. You hear someone on your tail. You turn to look but can only see their silhouette. Can you match the silhouette to one of the people you met earlier?

If you think it's Moriarty, turn to entry 50.

If you think it's Christa Belle, turn to entry 172.

If you think it's Stapleton, turn to entry 113.

If you think it's Peterson, turn to entry 8.

164 That is not the correct name. Lose a life and go back to entry 103.

165 You won't find Moriarty's hideout there, I'm sorry to say. Lose a life and race back to entry 190.

You worked out the message: Look under the steps. Under the steps leading down into the cell, you find an opening in the stonework containing a bunch of keys. Which key matches the chalk outline?

If your answer is A, turn to entry 6.

If your answer is B, turn to entry 111.

If your answer is C, turn to entry 109.

If your answer is D, turn to entry 179.

167 You have failed to identify the silhouette. Lose a life and go back to entry 177.

168 That was not the correct door. Lose a life and go back to entry 15.

169 You go through the door and it quickly closes and locks behind you. You are in a prison cell. Moriarty is watching you through the bars. You've fallen into his trap! "To win your freedom," he says, "you must solve a series of tests." For your first test, see if you can work out what pattern will complete this sequence so you can proceed to the next room.

A   B   C   D

If your answer is A, turn to entry 58.

If your answer is B, turn to entry 145.

If your answer is C, turn to entry 46.

If your answer is D, turn to entry 201.

170 Those are NOT the numbers in Moriarty's head! Lose a life and go back to entry 159.

171 Look again! You chose a name that's in the wordsearch puzzle. Lose a life and go back to entry 193.

172 You failed to identify the silhouette. Lose a life and ski back to entry 163.

173

When you reach Meiringen, you see an elderly lady and introduce yourself as a detective. You ask her if she knows of anyone who can guide you to Mount Reichenbach. She says she does, but she wishes to test your skills first by asking you to work out the guide's name. She hands you a piece of paper with three possible names and a number on it. You realize this is a code where each letter has been substituted for a number. Can you crack the code and unscramble the letters to reveal the name? The code is 20-19-5-18-8-18-5-5-9-14-25-12.

If you think the man's name is Heine Schmidt, turn to entry 34.

If you think the man's name is Henri Garnier, turn to entry 156.

If you think the man's name is Henry Steiler, turn to entry 183.

174
That does not match the shape of the key, and now your pursuers are closing in. Lose a life and hurry back to entry 29.

175
That is not what the message says. Lose a life and go back to entry 180.

176
You have failed to identify Peterson. Lose a life, go back to entry 187, and recheck those clues!

177 Good work! You got the coordinates right. The mountain must be in Switzerland or northern Italy.

Suddenly, the cell door opens and a silhouette appears at the top of the staircase. Do you recognize this man? What is his name?

If you think it's Moriarty, turn to entry 59.
If you think it's Moran, turn to entry 167.
If you think it's Peterson, turn to entry 100.

178 The note you chose was real, not fake. Lose a life and buy yourself a return ticket to entry 144.

179 That key does not match the chalk outline, unfortunately. Lose a life and go back to entry 166.

180

You correctly identify the book as *Wuthering Heights*, a novel by Emily Brontë (printed under the pen name Ellis Bell). You find the message inside, and it's in code. Can you work out what it means?

WUTHERING HEIGHTS

ELLIS BELL

Which answer is correct?

Café Amelia, Rue de Rimini, Thursday at six, turn to entry 63.

Café Aurora, Rue de Berlin, Saturday at one, turn to entry 104.

Café Angela, Rue de Rivoli, Tomorrow at ten, turn to entry 107.

Café Andrea, Rue de Roma, Friday at two, turn to entry 175.

181 I'm afraid you chose the wrong location for the secret passage. Lose a life and go back to entry 200.

182 You chose the wrong train. Lose a life and steam back to entry 82.

183

You correctly work out Henry Steiler's name and the elderly lady tells you where you can find him. He agrees to lead you up into the mountains. You reach a point where the path splits into four, and he stops. He can't remember which path to take. There are four sets of footprints in the snow. Which of these footprints matches Christa Belle's?

184 That is not the quickest route to Moriarty's hideout. Lose a life and go back to entry 36.

185 You picked the wrong boat! Lose a life and sail back to entry 8.

186 That is not what the message reveals. Lose a life and go back to entry 131.

A   B   C   D

If your answer is A, turn to entry 98.

If your answer is B, turn to entry 21.

If your answer is C, turn to entry 195.

If your answer is D, turn to entry 60.

187

You take the quickest train to Paris. You have arranged to meet with Peterson, a spy who has been helping you track Moriarty, at the railway station. You've never met Peterson before, and you do not know if they are male or female. Can you identify Peterson from the crowd?

This is what you know about Peterson:

- They always travel alone.
- They prefer not to wear a hat.
- They carry a briefcase.
- They have a full head of hair.

If the correct person has the label A, turn to entry 105.
If the correct person has the label B, turn to entry 97.
If the correct person has the label C, turn to entry 176.

188
You got your symbols wrong. Lose a life and recalculate your way back to entry 117.

189
You have failed to decode the message. Lose a life and return to entry 120.

190

You find a mistake in the emblem of Britannia, proving the banknotes are fake. Her suitcase also contains a map of part of central Rome. A secret location—which must be Moriarty's hideout—is given as a series of clues. Can you work out where it is?

- It runs directly to the Colosseum.
- It is west of S. Maria Maggiore.
- It has a junction with Via Nazionale.

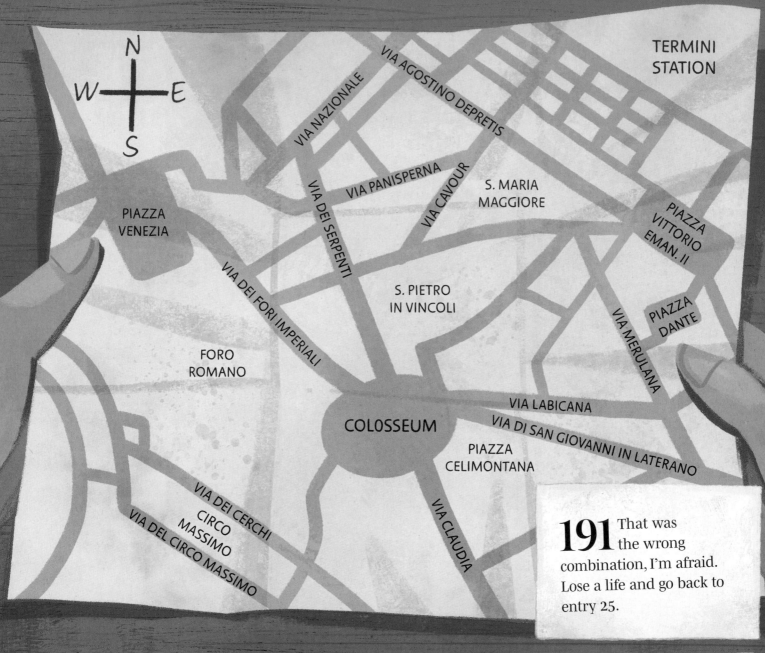

If your answer is Via dei Fori Imeriali, turn to entry 108.
If your answer is Via Agostino Depretis, turn to entry 165.
If your answer is Via dei Serpenti, turn to entry 141.

191
That was the wrong combination, I'm afraid. Lose a life and go back to entry 25.

192
You chose the wrong rope to climb down! Lose a life and haul yourself back to entry 152.

You enter the correct combination and move to the next room. Here, you find a list of names: Belle, Moriarty, Peterson, Moran. A guard hands you a grid of letters. Moriarty's voice crackles through a speaker. He says: "Look up, down, and diagonally. Which one of these names cannot be found in here?"

M	B	C	U	P	A	I	M	Y	N
D	O	M	B	E	L	H	A	R	A
A	P	F	O	P	S	Y	C	K	R
P	E	Y	A	R	E	P	I	T	O
U	T	H	L	M	I	T	O	L	M
I	E	P	B	D	Y	A	E	U	O
C	R	I	E	W	P	E	R	S	I
S	T	U	L	A	H	M	A	T	R
R	M	O	L	I	T	U	N	M	Y
Y	S	R	E	S	N	O	D	I	A

If you think it's Belle, turn to entry 171.

If you think it's Moriarty, turn to entry 27.

If you think it's Peterson, turn to entry 159.

If you think it's Moran, turn to entry 123.

194 You chose the wrong door! Lose a life and go back to entry 134.

195 Those footprints did not match Christa Belle's. Lose a life and hike back to entry 183.

You follow the accomplice, Colonel Moran, into another room where he appears to vanish through a solid wall. There are four panels in the wall. You think there might be a secret door in one of the panels. You search the panels to see if one is different from the rest.

A   **B**   **C**

Which panel is different?

If your answer is A, turn to entry 91.

If your answer is B, turn to entry 125.

If your answer is C, turn to entry 134.

197 That was not the correct symbol. Lose a life and go back to entry 75.

198 That was not the correct answer to complete the sequence. Lose a life and go back to entry 159.

199 That is the wrong address. Lose a life and mail yourself back to entry 18.

200

You successfully work out Peterson's number and call him. He tells you the key you need is in the kitchen. According to the map, you can access the kitchen via the bedroom, but the bedroom door is locked. You hear Christa Belle approaching from the entrance hall. You need a quick escape. There's a secret passage from the library to the kitchen. Check the map. Can you see which set of shelves it's hiding behind?

A

B

BEDROOM

C

If you think it's behind A, turn to entry 181.

If you think it's behind B, turn to entry 148.

If you think it's behind C, turn to entry 42.

201 That pattern does not complete the sequence, I'm afraid. Lose a life and go back to entry 169.

202 I'm sorry to say that's not the fake note. Lose a life and spend your way back to entry 144.

203 That man is not the closest match to the silhouette. Lose a life and head back to entry 72.

204

You put the pieces of the picture back together to reveal a building called the Colosseum. Thanks to the message on the picture, you know that Moriarty is here. In which European city is the Colosseum?

If you think it's Rome, turn to entry 82.
If you think it's Athens, turn to entry 142.
If you think it's Madrid, turn to entry 35.
If you think it's Berlin, turn to entry 96.

205
That route will not get you through the maze. Lose a life and find your way back to entry 155.

206
I'm afraid that's not the right door. Lose a life and go back to entry 134.

207
You have failed to identify the correct door. Lose a life and head back to entry 15.